Get ready
for more
LAUGHS!

NATIONAL GEOGRAPHIC
KIDS

Just Joking 2

300 hilarious jokes about everything, including tongue twisters, riddles, and more!

NATIONAL GEOGRAPHIC

WASHINGTON, D.C.

Snow leopards are rare cats that live in the mountains of Central Asia.

HA! HA! HA! HA! HA! HA! HA! HA! HA! HA! HA! HA! HA! HA! HA! HA!

5

6

The orangutan is the world's largest tree-dwelling animal.

Say this fast three times:

Fred threw thirty-three free throws.

Q What is the best thing to put into a pie?

A Your teeth.

7

Q What colors would you paint the sun and the wind?

A The sun rose and the wind blue.

BOY Are caterpillars good to eat?

FATHER No. Why do you ask?

BOY You had one in your salad, but it's gone now.

Q What do farmers give their sweethearts for Valentine's Day?

IT'S LOVE   MY BABY

A A hog and a kiss.

Q Why is **slippery** pavement like music?

A If you don't C sharp, you'll B flat!

8

Madagascar is home to about 150 chameleon species, including this Boettger's chameleon.

9

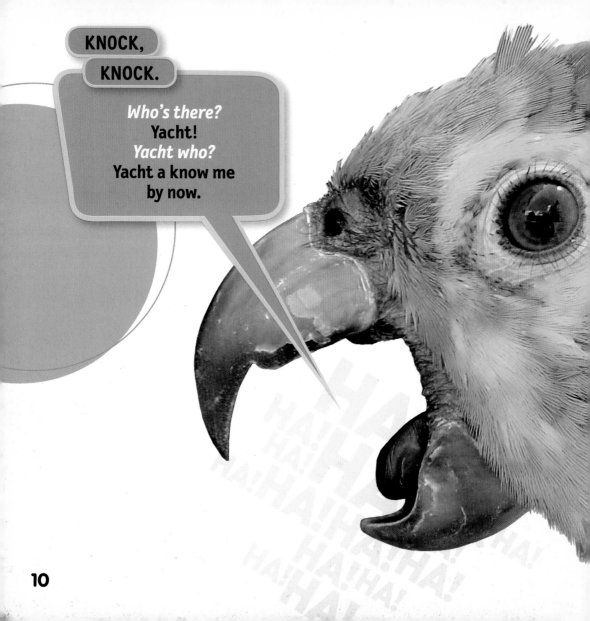

HA! HA! HA! HA! HA! HA! HA! HA! HA! HA! HA! HA! HA!

Parrots can live for
more than 70 years.

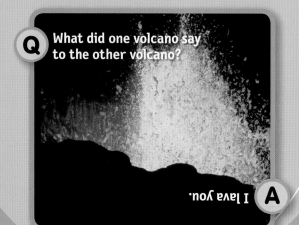

Q What did one volcano say to the other volcano?

A I lava you.

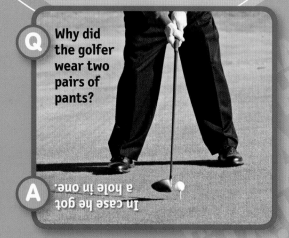

Q Why did the golfer wear two pairs of pants?

A In case he got a hole in one.

12

Parrot snakes are found in southern Mexico and South America.

KNOCK,

KNOCK.

Who's there?
Says.
Says who?
Says me,
that's who!

13

Flamingos use mouthfuls of mud to build their nests.

Why are **flamingos** always happy?

Because they are never blue.

TONGUE TWISTER!

Say this fast three times:

Kent sent Trent to the tent.

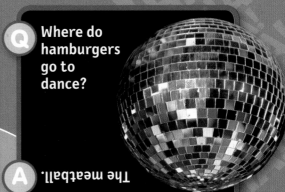

Q Where do hamburgers go to dance?

A The meatball.

Q Why did the kid put ice in his aunt's bed?

A He wanted to make auntifreeze.

Q What **room** has no floor, windows, or doors?

A A mushroom!

Bob brought back from the

blue balloons big bazaar.

A hippopotamus can hold its breath underwater for up to five minutes.

KNOCK, KNOCK.

Who's there?
Mary Lee.
Mary Lee who?
Mary Lee down the stream.

18

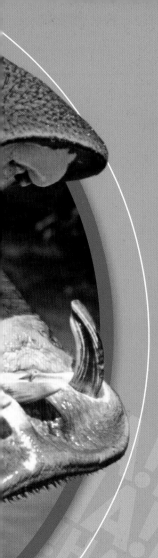

 Q From what word can you take away *the whole* and still have *some left?*

A Wholesome.

TONGUE TWISTER!

Say this fast three times:

Old oily Olly oils old oily autos.

TONGUE TWISTER!

Say this fast three times:

Skunks sat on a stump and the stump stunk.

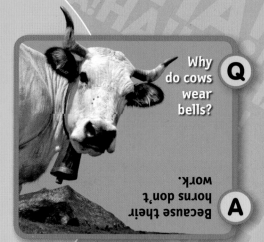

Q Why do cows wear bells?

A Because their horns don't work.

Q What can a whole orange do that a half an orange can't do?

A Look 'round.

Q What goes **up** but never comes down?

A Your age.

20

KNOCK, KNOCK.

Who's there?
Xavier.
Xavier who?
Xavier breath and open that door.

This bird, called a bee-eater, can capture prey while flying.

Box turtles burrow up to two feet into the ground for hibernation.

23

Hawaiian monk seals weigh up to 600 pounds (272 kg)—as much as a small horse!

KNOCK, KNOCK.

Who's there?
Sam.
Sam who?
Sam person who knocked before!

24

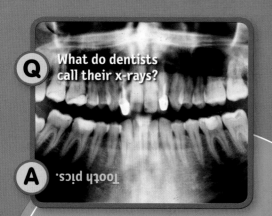

Q What do dentists call their x-rays?

A Tooth pics.

Q What did **Robin Hood** have when the arrow fired at him missed?

An-arrow escape!

A

Q What happened to the cat who swallowed a ball of wool?

Q She had mittens.

Q What happened after the girl drank eight sodas?

A She burped seven up.

DOCTOR:
Nurse, did you take the patient's temperature?

NURSE:
Why, no, doctor. Is it missing?

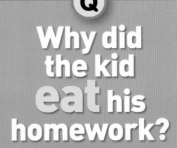

Q

Why did the kid **eat** his homework?

A Because his teacher said it was a piece of cake.

Q

What did the **grape** do when it got stepped on?

A It let out a little wine.

What is a witch's favorite subject in school? **Q**

A Spelling.

Chimpanzee calls can be heard a mile away.

KNOCK, KNOCK.

Who's there?
Cousin.
Cousin who?
Cousin stead of opening the door, you're making me stand here.

27

It takes up to 26 hours for a hen to lay just one egg.

Why do
hens lay
eggs?

Because they break if they drop them.

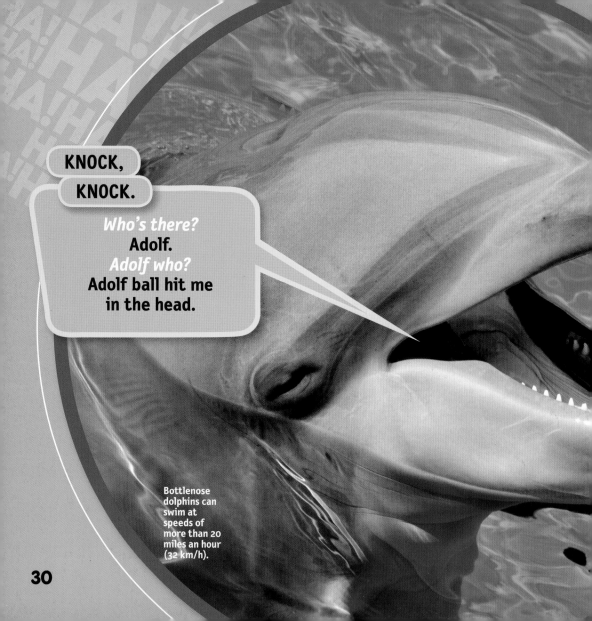

KNOCK, KNOCK.

Who's there?
Adolf.
Adolf who?
Adolf ball hit me in the head.

Bottlenose dolphins can swim at speeds of more than 20 miles an hour (32 km/h).

30

Q

What is the richest kind of air?

A

Millionaire.

Q What should you take along on a trek through the desert?

A A thirst-aid kit.

31

Q Why did the farmer's wife chase the chickens out of the yard?

A They were using fowl language.

Q What kind of car does a rich cow drive?

A A Cattle-lac!

SUE: Look—there's a baby snake.

LOU: How do you know it's a baby?

SUE: You can tell by its rattle!

Q What did the **hat** say to the **hat rack?**

A "You stay here. I'll go on ahead."

Black bears "clack" their teeth when frightened.

33

34

Zebras make braying, barking, and snorting sounds.

How much does it cost a
pirate
to get his ears pierced?

A buck an ear.

Q Why was the farmer famous?

A He was out standing in his field.

TONGUE TWISTER!

Say this fast three times:

Shelter for six sick scenic sightseers.

Q

How did the **tree** feel after the beaver left?

A "Gnawed," so good.

Q Where do snowmen put their Web pages?

A On the Winter-net.

37

Q What sports are trains good at?

A Track events.

Q

What did the **wind** say to the **screen door?**

"Just passing through."

Gray wolves consume up to 20 pounds (9 kg) of meat in one meal.

HA! HA! HA! HA! HA! HA! HA! HA! HA! HA!

39

Can canned cla

Clams can live in fresh water or salt water, buried up to two feet (0.6 m) deep in the sandy bottom.

ms can clams?

Merino sheep originated in Spain and are known for producing fine wool.

Where did the sheep get its hair cut?

At the baa-baa shop.

Q What is the elephant's favorite vegetable?

A Squash.

Q Which hand would you use to pick up a dangerous snake?

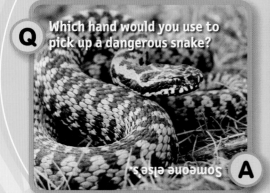

A Someone else's.

A police officer saw a woman in her car with a penguin. The officer said, "It's against the law to have that penguin in your car! Take it to the zoo."

The next day the police officer saw the same woman in her car with the same penguin. He said, "I told you to take that penguin to the zoo!"

The woman replied, "I did. He liked it so much, today we're going to the beach!"

KNOCK, KNOCK.

Who's there?
Mikey.
Mikey who?
Mikey doesn't fit
in the keyhole.

44

Q Why did the pony have a sore throat?

A He was a little horse.

Caimans are related to alligators.

Q

Why do elephants do well in school?

Because they have a lot of gray matter.

45

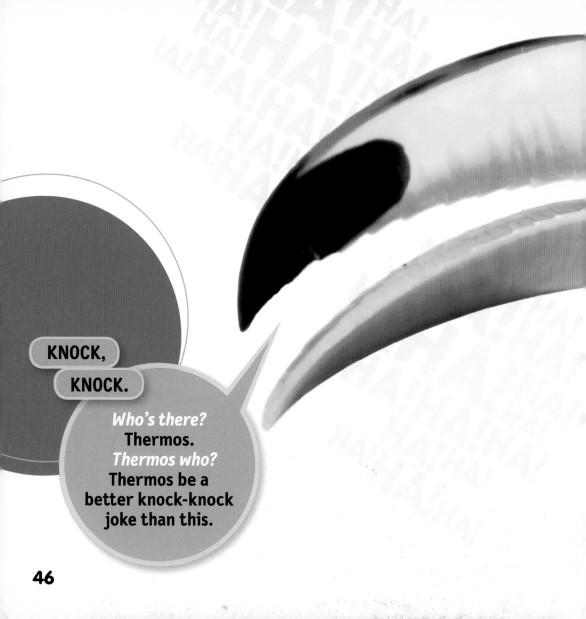

KNOCK, KNOCK.

Who's there?
Thermos.
Thermos who?
Thermos be a better knock-knock joke than this.

HA!
HA! HA!
HA! HA!
HA!HA!HA!
HA!HA!HA!
HA!HA!

A toucan does not
have a large bill when
it hatches; it takes a
few months for its bill
to become full size.

47

Q What part of the fish weighs the most?

A The scales.

Q What would you have if Batman and Robin were run over by stampeding cattle?

A Flatman and Ribbon.

Q

Why is the letter *G* scary?

A It turns a host into a ghost.

Q What did the one lightning bolt say to the other lightning bolt?

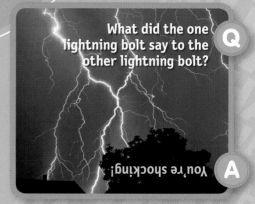

A You're shocking!

Grasshoppers smell with organs located on their antennae.

What did the **grasshopper** say when it hit the **windshield?**

"If I had the guts, I'd do it again."

Atlantic puffins breed in the North Atlantic, building nests atop rocky seaside cliffs.

Q What athlete can jump higher than a building?

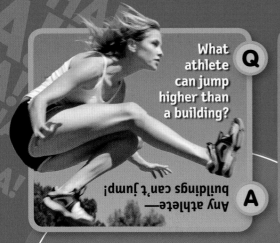

A Any athlete—buildings can't jump!

Q What washes up on very small beaches?

A Micro-waves.

Q What would you do if a rhino came after you at 60 miles an hour?

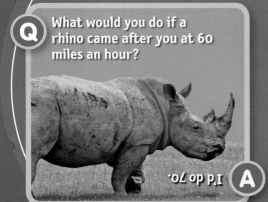

A I'd do 70.

Q What did the **envelope** say to the **stamp?**

A "Stick to me and we'll go places!"

51

There are more than 45 recognized rabbit breeds in the United States alone.

What do you call a a rabbit who is really cool?

A hip hopper.

53

Q What do you call a goat's beard?

A A goatee.

The buffy fish owl sometimes uses another bird's empty nest for itself.

TONGUE TWISTER!

Say this fast three times:

Walter wants **winter weather.**

Q Do **zombies** eat popcorn with their **fingers?**

A No—they eat the fingers separately.

Say this fast three times:

Dick kicks sticky bricks.

Q What color is a **burp?**

A Burple.

Q Why do dogs run in circles?

A Because it's hard to run in squares.

56

SOCCER PLAYER: Check it out—another straight-A report card.

TENNIS PLAYER: How do you do so well in school?

SOCCER PLAYER: I'm always using my head.

58

Ducks waddle because their feet are positioned close to their rear ends.

59

In a cold climate, a raccoon often doubles its body weight to prepare to sleep through the winter.

60

VOICE ON TELEPHONE: I'm afraid Karen won't be at school today.

PRINCIPAL: Who's calling?

VOICE: It's my mom.

Oops!

Say this fast three times:

Three free-thinking frogs think friendly thoughts.

Q

What kind of driver **never** gets a **ticket?**

A screwdriver.

A

Q What kind of dinosaur is never late?

A "pronto-saur-us."

A

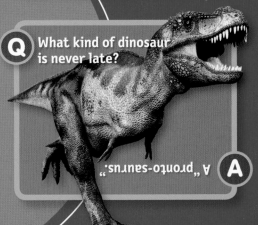

61

Q Why did the **penny,** but not the quarter, jump off the cliff?

A The quarter had more cents.

TONGUE TWISTER!

Say this fast three times:

Bobby Blue blew big blue bubbles.

Orcas are also called killer whales.

KNOCK, KNOCK.

Who's there?
Dots.
Dots who?
Dot's for me to know and you to find out.

63

What do you get
when you cross
a **snake**
and a
Lego set?

A boa constructor.

64

There are about 2,700 species of snakes, but only about 375 species, including this diamondback, are venomous.

Pelicans, such as this great white pelican, use their elastic pouches to catch fish.

KNOCK, KNOCK.

Who's there?
Hawaii.
Hawaii who?
I'm fine.
Hawaii you?

Say this fast three times:

A shapeless sash sags slowly.

Q Why did the cheetah refuse to bathe in dishwashing detergent?

A He didn't want to come out spotless.

Q How is a **baseball team** similar to a **muffin?**

A They both depend on the batter.

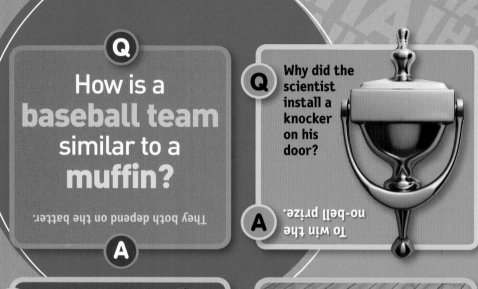

Q Why did the scientist install a knocker on his door?

A To win the no-bell prize.

Q What do dogs do after they're through with obedience school?

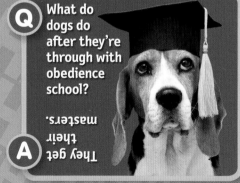

A They get their masters.

Q What did the carpet say to the floor?

A "Don't worry. I'm on top of everything."

68

Say this fast three times:

Fussy Freddie flings food furiously.

Bats are
the only flying
mammals.

71

Harp seal mothers can identify their young by scent alone.

KNOCK, KNOCK.

Who's there?
Albie.
Albie who?
Albie out here if you need me.

A duck walks into the drugstore to buy some lip balm. The cashier asks the duck, "Cash or charge?" The duck says, "Just put it on my bill."

Why did the man run around his **bed?**

A To catch up on his sleep.

PATIENT:

What is the best way to prevent diseases caused by biting insects?

DOCTOR:

Don't bite any!

73

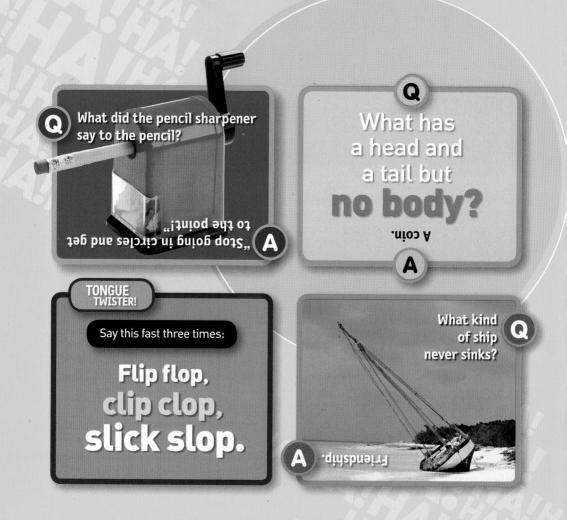

Q What did the pencil sharpener say to the pencil?

A "Stop going in circles and get to the point!"

Q What has a head and a tail but **no body?**

A A coin.

TONGUE TWISTER!

Say this fast three times:

Flip flop, clip clop, slick slop.

Q What kind of ship never sinks?

A Friendship.

74

Two thieves robbing an apartment hear the owner coming home.

"Quick, jump out the window," says the first robber.

"Are you crazy? We're on the 13th floor!" says the second robber.

The first one replies, "This is no time to be superstitious!"

Swan swam over the sea. Swim, swan, swim.

Swans mate for life.

Swan swam back again. Well swum, swan!

A serval's hearing is so sensitive it can hear prey moving underground.

KNOCK, KNOCK.

Who's there?
Adore.
Adore who?
Adore stands between us. Open up!

Q How do you make a hot dog stand?

A Take away its chair.

TONGUE TWISTER!

Say this fast three times:

Flora's freshly fried fish.

79

Q Why do bees have sticky hair?

A Because they have honeycombs.

Say this fast three times:

Mix, miss, mix!

Say this fast three times:

An ape hates grape cakes.

Q What is the **hottest** letter in the alphabet?

A B, because it makes oil . . . Boil!

Donkeys are also called burros.

KNOCK, KNOCK.

Who's there?
Stopwatch.
Stopwatch who?
Stopwatch you're doing and open this door.

81

Cats can make more than 100 vocal sounds.

83

Chameleons can move one eye at a time.

KNOCK, KNOCK.

Who's there?
Voodoo.
Voodoo who?
Voodoo you think you are?

Q What did one **flea** say to the other as they left the restaurant?

A "Shall we walk or take a dog?"

Q What do you say when a balloon pops?

A "May you rest in pieces."

Q What books did the owl like?

A Hoot-dunits!

Q What has four **wheels** and flies?

A A garbage truck.

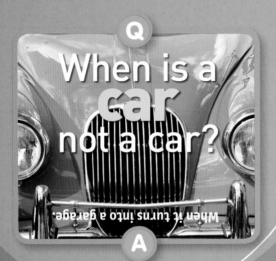

Q When is a **car** not a car?

A When it turns into a garage.

Q Why did the whale cross the road?

A To get to the other tide.

The Mugger crocodile can grow up to 16 feet (4.9 m) long—about the length of an SUV!

KNOCK, KNOCK.

Who's there?
Theodore.
Theodore who?
Theodore wasn't open, so I knocked.

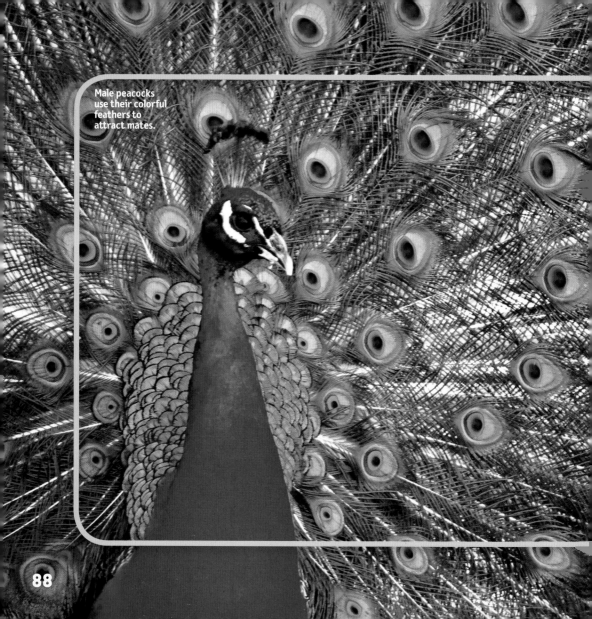

Male peacocks use their colorful feathers to attract mates.

Where does a
peacock
go when it loses its
tail?

A retail store.

A man rushes into the doctor's office and shouts, "Doctor! I think I'm shrinking!" The doctor calmly responds, "Now, settle down. You'll just have to be a little patient."

Q

Why was the archaeologist upset?

A

His job was in ruins.

Q

Why did the gum cross the road?

A

Because it was stuck to the chicken's foot.

Q

Why are elephants wrinkled?

A

Have you ever tried to iron one?

TONGUE TWISTER!

Say this fast three times:

Bob's big black bath brush broke.

Q There are two farms next to each other. One is in Canada and one is in the United States. A rooster runs from the farm in Canada to the farm in the U.S. and lays an egg. So which country does the egg actually belong to?

A Neither. Roosters don't lay eggs.

Q How do **mermaids** keep in contact with each other?

A They use their shell phones.

Q How do you get rid of a boomerang?

A Throw it down a one-way street.

An upset man calls the fire department to report a fire in his neighborhood. The dispatcher asks him, "How do we get there?" The man replies, "Don't you still have those big red trucks?"

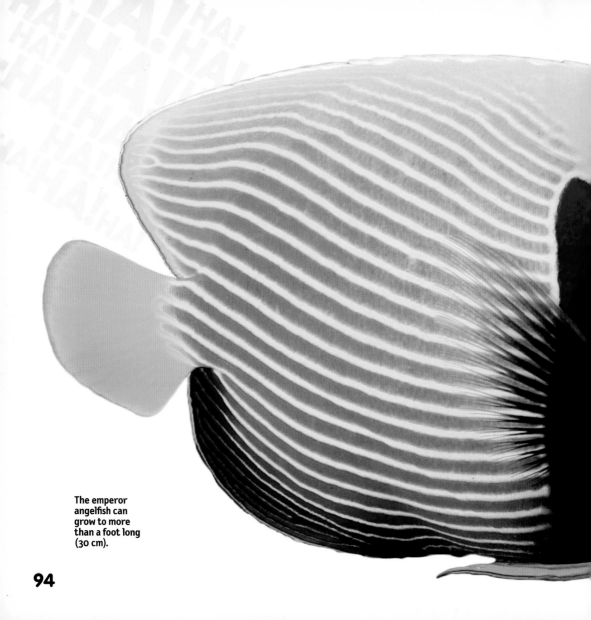

The emperor angelfish can grow to more than a foot long (30 cm).

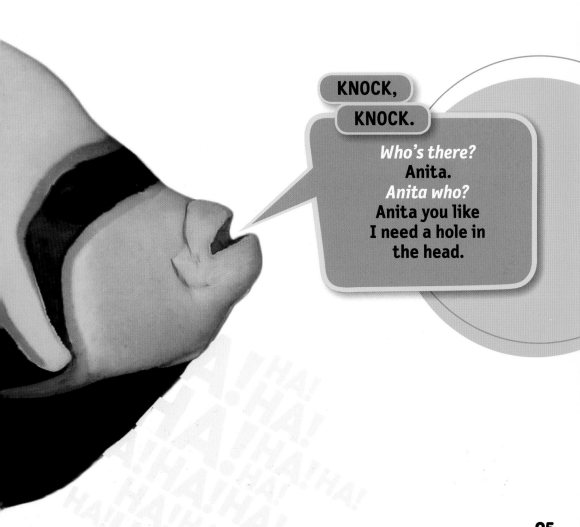

95

Fred fed Ted bread.

Ted fed Fred bread.

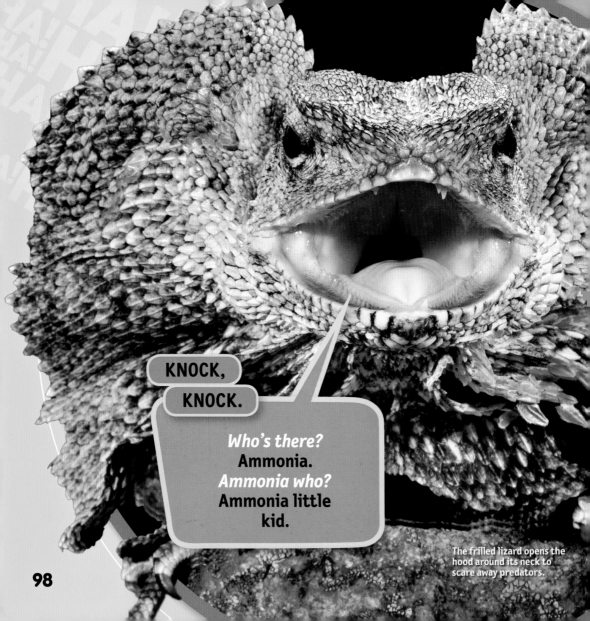

KNOCK, KNOCK.

Who's there?
Ammonia.
Ammonia who?
Ammonia little kid.

The frilled lizard opens the hood around its neck to scare away predators.

What jam can't be eaten on toast? Q

A A traffic jam.

Q

What weighs
5,000 lb.
and wears
glass slippers?

Cinderelephant.

A

99

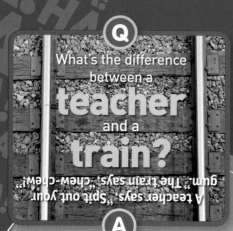

Q What's the difference between a **teacher** and a **train?**

A A teacher says, "Spit out your gum." The train says, "chew-chew!"

TONGUE TWISTER!

Say this fast three times:

Tiny turtles trotted to the track.

Q What kind of birds stick together?

A Vel-crows.

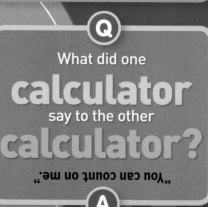

Q What did one **calculator** say to the other **calculator?**

A "You can count on me."

Ostriches are the world's largest birds.

KNOCK, KNOCK.

Who's there?
Isaiah.
Isaiah who?
Isaiah nothing until you open this door.

Which letters are not

OPQUSTUVWXYZ
MLKJGIHFEDCBA
OPQUSTUVWXYZ
MLKJGIHFEDCBA

in the
alphabet?

The ones in the mail!

OPQUSTUVWXYZ
MLKJGIHFEDCBA

Red-knobbed hornbills are native to Sulawesi, an island in Indonesia, and other nearby islands.

KNOCK, KNOCK.

Who's there?
Baby owl.
Baby owl who?
Baby owl see you when you open the door.

Q Why did the cookie go to the hospital?

A Because it felt crummy.

Q Why was **6** afraid of **7**?

A Because 7 8 9.

Q What has **four** legs but can't **walk?**

A A table.

Q Why do seagulls fly over the sea?

A Because if they flew over the bay they would be bagels.

105

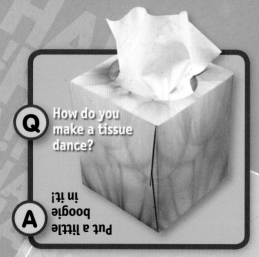

Q How do you make a tissue dance?

A Put a little boogie in it!

Q What has **four eyes** but no **face?**

Mississippi

A

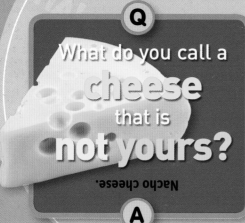

Q What do you call a **cheese** that is **not yours?**

Nacho cheese.

A

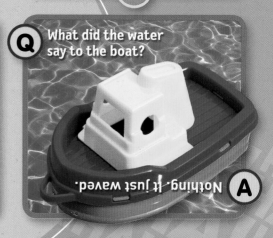

Q What did the water say to the boat?

Nothing. It just waved.

A

What kind of
bow
can't be tied?

A rainbow!

KNOCK, KNOCK.

Who's there?
Alpaca.
Alpaca who?
Alpaca a trunk,
you pack a suitcase.

108

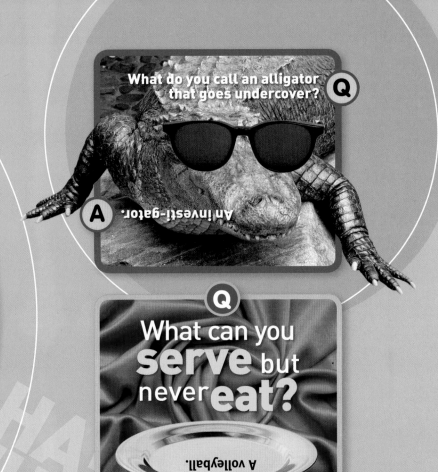

Q What do you call an alligator that goes undercover?

A An investi-gator.

Q What can you **serve** but never **eat**?

A A volleyball.

Koalas spend up to 18 hours a day napping.

109

110

Seals mostly eat fish, squid, mollusks, and crustaceans.

Q What did one plate say to the other plate?

A "Lunch is on me."

Q

What has no **fingers** but has many **rings?**

A tree.

A

The llama is a South American relative of the camel.

KNOCK, KNOCK.

Who's there?
Botany.
Botany who?
Botany good books lately?

113

Smelly shoes and

socks shock Sis.

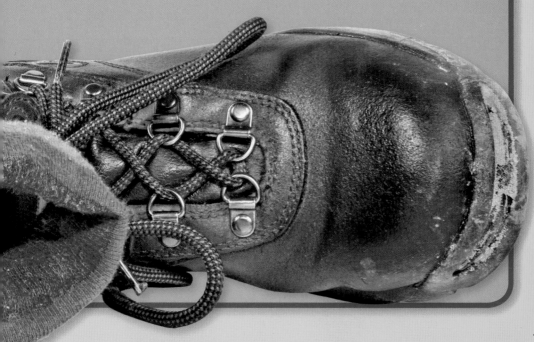

Male goats are called billies; female goats are called nannies.

KNOCK, KNOCK.

Who's there?
Clara.
Clara who?
Clara space at the table.

116

Say this fast three times:

A cricket critic.

Q Why did the woman leave her purse open when she went outside?

A Because she expected some change in the weather.

117

TONGUE TWISTER!

Say this fast three times:

A glowing gleam glowing green.

Q What do you feed a noisy dog?

A Hush puppies.

Q What did the banana do when the monkey chased it?

A The banana split.

Q Why did the watchmaker enjoy his vacation?

A Because he learned to unwind.

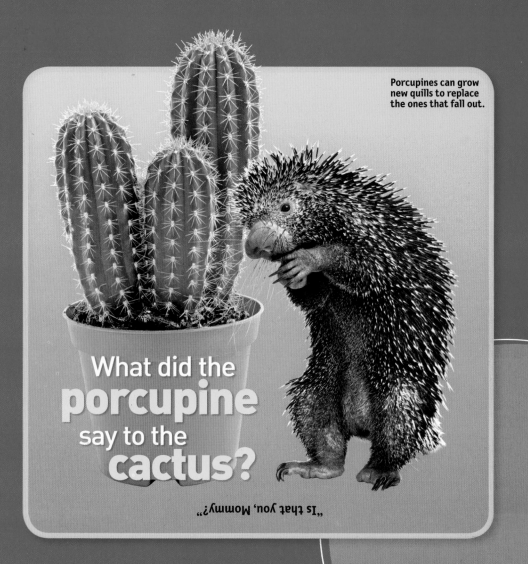

Porcupines can grow new quills to replace the ones that fall out.

What did the **porcupine** say to the **cactus?**

"Is that you, Mommy?"

119

120

White tigers have a rare gene that changes the color of their fur.

Guernsey cows like this one are bred for milk, not meat.

KNOCK, KNOCK.

Who's there?
Colleen.
Colleen who?
Colleen up this mess out here.

On the first day of class, the teacher asked all trouble-makers to stand up. After a few moments of silence, a shy little girl stood up. "Are you a troublemaker?" the teacher asked. "No," replied the girl. "I just hate to see you standing there all by yourself."

Q Why did the bowler move to the ocean?

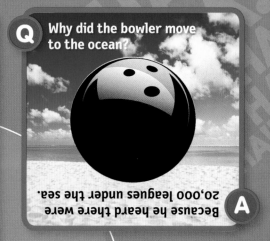

A Because he heard there were 20,000 leagues under the sea.

Q Why was the **fisherman** angry at the **computer?**

A He wasn't getting any bytes.

Q Which tree doesn't play checkers?

A The chess nut.

Q How many days of the week start with the letter *T*?

A Four. Tuesday, Thursday, today, and tomorrow.

January 2012

Sun	Mon	Tue	Wed	Thu	Fri	Sat
1	2	3	4	5	6	7
8	9	10	11	12	13	14
15	16	17	18	19	20	21
22	23	24	25	26	27	28
29	30	31				

TONGUE TWISTER!

Say this fast three times:

Fish sauce shop.

Q What goes snap, crackle, pop?

A A firefly with a short circuit.

124

Buy blue blueberry biscuits before bedtime.

There are more chickens on Earth than people.

What do you get if you cross a chicken with a skunk?

Skunk spray can travel as far as ten feet (3 m).

A fowl smell.

KNOCK, KNOCK.

Who's there?
Beets.
Beets who?
Beets me!

Sea otters float in
groups of up to 100.

128

Q

Why couldn't the pirate play cards?

A Because he was sitting on the deck.

TONGUE TWISTER!

Say this fast three times:

Upper roller, lower roller.

PATIENT: Doctor, Doctor! I've lost
my memory!
DOCTOR: When did this happen?
PATIENT: When did what happen?

Q Have you heard the rumor
about the butter?

A I'd better not tell you.
It might spread.

Q What do you do with
a blue whale?

A Try to cheer him up.

130

Tree squirrels are sometimes called "living fossils" because they look basically the same as they did five million years ago.

KNOCK, KNOCK.

Who's there?
Tom Sawyer.
Tom Sawyer who?
Tom sawyer underpants.

131

A snail secretes liquid that hardens to form its shell.

132

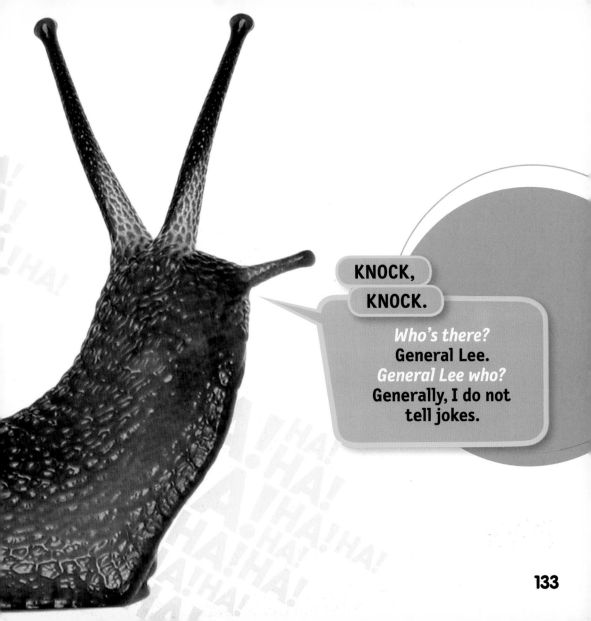

133

Say this fast three times:

Ten toothsome tarts tempted Tom's tranquility.

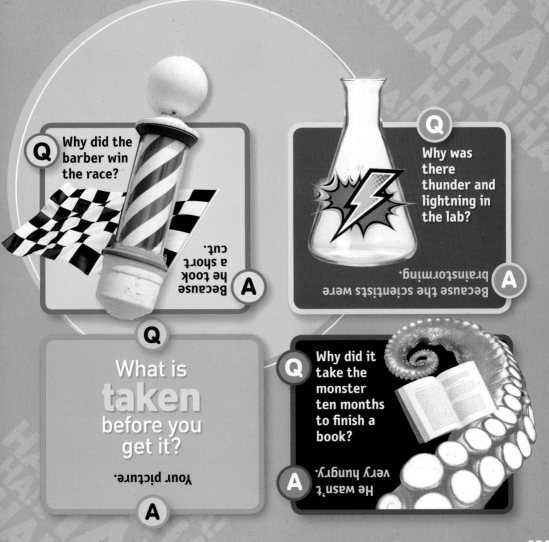

Q Why did the barber win the race?

A Because he took a short cut.

Q Why was there thunder and lightning in the lab?

A Because the scientists were brainstorming.

Q What is **taken** before you get it?

A Your picture.

Q Why did it take the monster ten months to finish a book?

A He wasn't very hungry.

135

Say this fast three times:

Tie twine to three tree twigs.

Q Why should you take a **pencil** to bed?

A To draw the curtains!

136

KNOCK, KNOCK.

Who's there?
Dwayne.
Dwayne who?
Dwayne the bathtub,
I'm dwowning.

Red pandas live
in the trees in
mountain forests
of Asia.

137

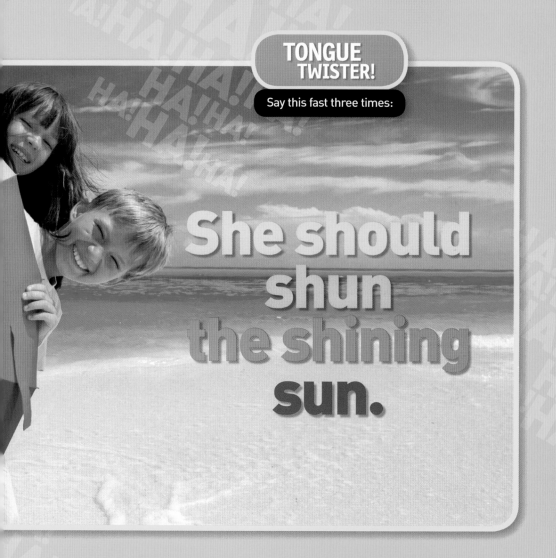

She should shun the shining sun.

Q What does a teddy bear put in his house?

A Fur-niture.

Q What season is it when you are on a trampoline?

A Spring time.

Q How many books can you put in an empty backpack?

A One! After that it's not empty.

Q What happens if you eat **yeast** and **shoe polish?**

A You'll rise and shine every morning.

HA! HA! HA! HA! HA! HA!

Q What
breaks
when you
say it?

A Silence.

Q What do teenage
geese suffer from?

A Goose pimples.

Q What gets
bigger
the more you
take away from it?

A A hole.

TONGUE TWISTER!

Say this fast three times:

Shave a
single
shingle thin.

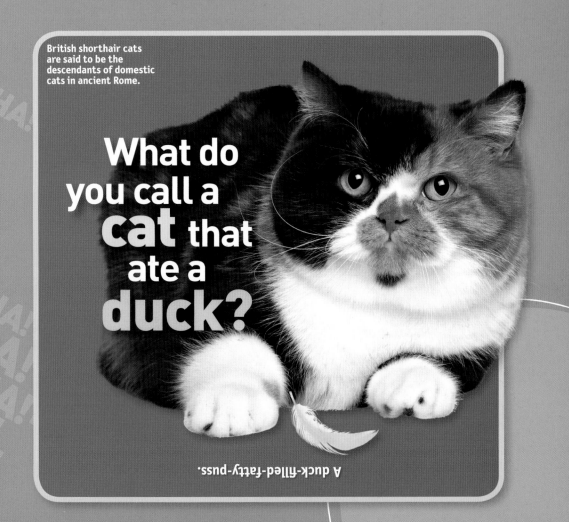

British shorthair cats are said to be the descendants of domestic cats in ancient Rome.

What do you call a **cat** that ate a **duck?**

A duck-filled-fatty-puss.

Female elephants
are called cows.

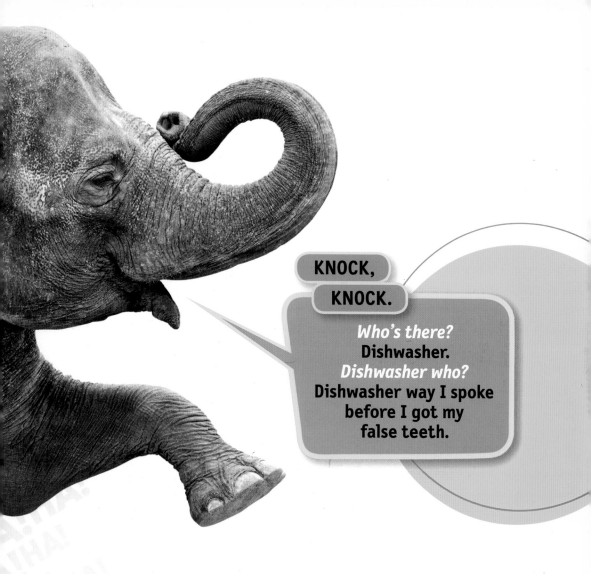

KNOCK, KNOCK.

Who's there?
Dishwasher.
Dishwasher who?
Dishwasher way I spoke before I got my false teeth.

145

What do you get when you cross an artist and a policeman?

A brush with the law.

KNOCK, KNOCK.

Who's there?
Ketchup.
Ketchup who?
Ketchup with
you soon!

148

Q

What did one elevator say to the other elevator?

A

"I think I'm coming down with something."

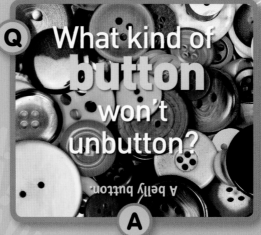

Q What kind of **button** won't unbutton?

A A belly button.

149

Q Why did Tony go out with a prune?

A Because he couldn't find a date.

Q Why don't they serve **chocolate** in prison?

A Because it makes you break out.

Q Why did the man with one **hand** cross the road?

A To get to the second-hand shop.

TONGUE TWISTER!

Say this fast three times:

Bad money, mad bunny.

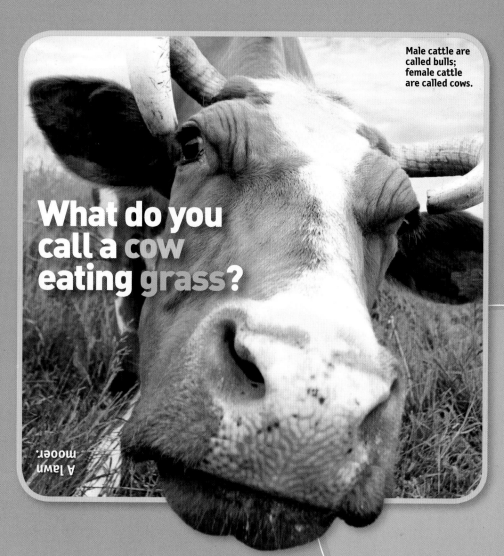

What do you call a cow eating grass?

Male cattle are called bulls; female cattle are called cows.

A lawn mooer.

151

Say this fast three times:

Three gray geese in the green grass grazing.

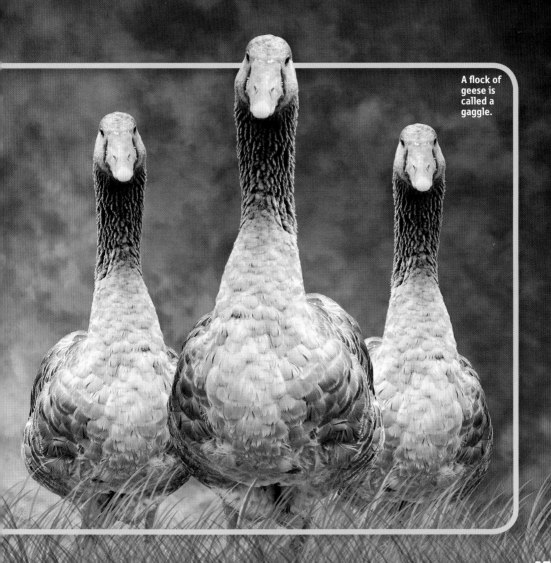

A flock of geese is called a gaggle.

153

KNOCK, KNOCK.

Who's there?
Danielle.
Danielle who?
Danielle at me!
It's not my fault!

The male brown booby makes whistling sounds; the female quacks and honks.

154

Q Why did the little boy put lipstick on his head?

A He wanted to make up his mind.

Q Did you hear what happened at the Laundromat last night?

A Three clothespins held up two shirts.

155

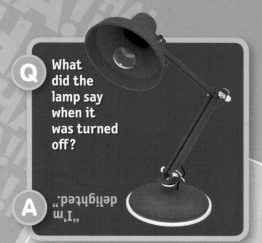

Q What did the lamp say when it was turned off?

A "I'm delighted."

Q What gets **older** but doesn't age?

A A portrait.

Q Why did the boy study in the **airplane?**

A He wanted a higher education.

Q What flower grows on your face?

A Two-lips.

Dromedary camels like this one have one hump; Bactrian camels have two humps.

157

Brown bears
are often called
grizzlies because
of their grayish,
or grizzled fur.

What did the
baby corn
say to the
mother corn?

"Where's pop-corn?"

160

Q What do you use to cut through giant waves?

A A sea saw.

Q What kind of can never needs a can opener?

A A pelican.

Q How do you make an ant out of breath?

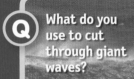

A Give it a p and make it pant.

Q What has a **neck** but cannot **swallow?**

A A bottle.

161

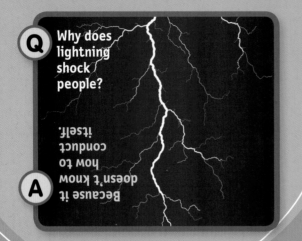

Q Why does lightning shock people?

A Because it doesn't know how to conduct itself.

Q Why shouldn't you tell a joke while ice skating?

A The ice might crack up!

162

Female iguanas lay about 30 to 50 eggs at once.

HA! HA! HA! HA! HA! HA! HA! HA! HA!

KNOCK, KNOCK.

Who's there?
Canoe.
Canoe who?
Canoe lend me some money?

163

What is the difference between a bottle of medicine and a doormat?

One is shaken up and taken, and the other is taken up and shaken.

Cheetahs only need to drink once every three to four days.

KNOCK, KNOCK.

Who's there?
Mara.
Mara who?
Mara, mara on the wall . . .

166

Say this fast three times:

The
sixth sick
sheikh's son
slept.

What do you call
seaside spooks? **Q**

A Ghost guards.

167

A horse's wide-set eyes allow it to spot danger more easily.

169

Q What walks around with its **head** on the ground?

A A nail in a shoe.

Q Why did the birdie go to the hospital?

A To get a tweetment.

Q What do you call a disastrous cat?

A A cat-astrophe.

Q Why is a traffic cop the strongest man in the world?

A He can stop a ten-ton truck with one hand!

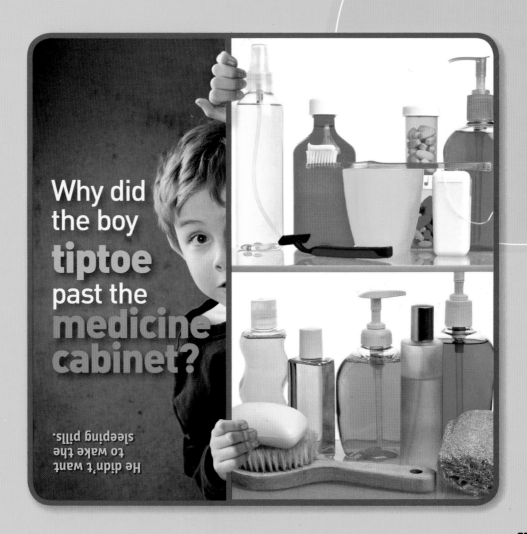

Why did
the boy
tiptoe
past the
**medicine
cabinet?**

He didn't want
to wake the
sleeping pills.

Why were the teacher's eyes always crossed?

He couldn't control his pupils.

Q When do you stop at green and go at red?

STOP

A When you're eating a watermelon.

Q Why was the broom late?

A It over swept.

Q What goes **up** when the rain comes **down?**

A An umbrella.

TONGUE TWISTER!

Say this fast three times:

Cinnamon aluminum linoleum.

Q What kind of cake do you get at the school cafeteria?

A A stomach-cake!

Q What **disappears** when you **stand up?**

Your lap.

A

TONGUE TWISTER!

Say this fast three times:

Tragedy strategy.

Q What did the dog say to the flea?

"You bug me!"

A

This ape is part chimpanzee, part bonobo.

KNOCK, KNOCK.

Who's there?
Formosa.
Formosa who?
Formosa the summer I was away on vacation.

175

Say this fast three times:

Six sharp smart sharks.

Great white sharks' favorite prey are sea lions and seals.

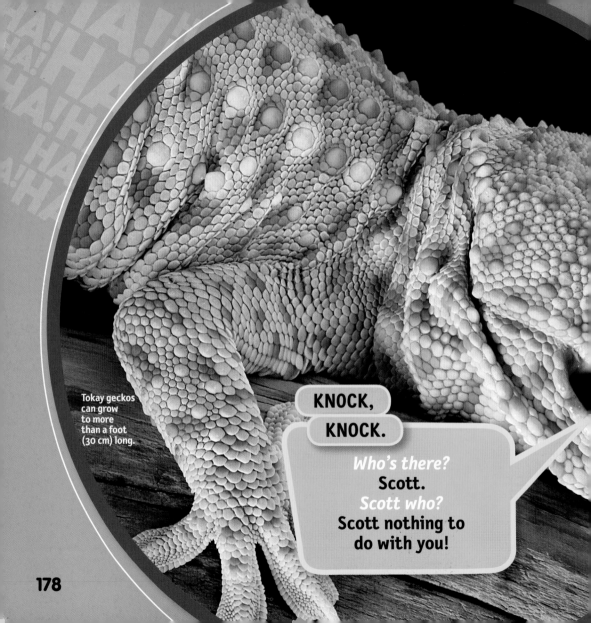

Tokay geckos can grow to more than a foot (30 cm) long.

178

TONGUE TWISTER!

Say this fast three times:

A bragging baker baked black bread.

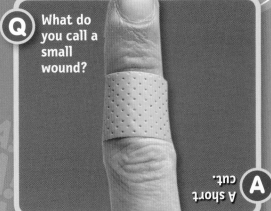

Q What do you call a small wound?

A A short cut.

179

A woman went to her psychiatrist and said, "Doctor, I want to talk to you about a problem. My husband thinks he's a refrigerator."

"Things could be worse," said the doctor. "That's a minor problem."

"It might be," replied the woman. "But he sleeps with his mouth open and the light keeps me awake!"

Say this fast three times:

Selfish shellfish.

Q

Why did the **computer** squeak?

Because someone stepped on its mouse.

A

Brown bears dig dens for winter hibernation.

181

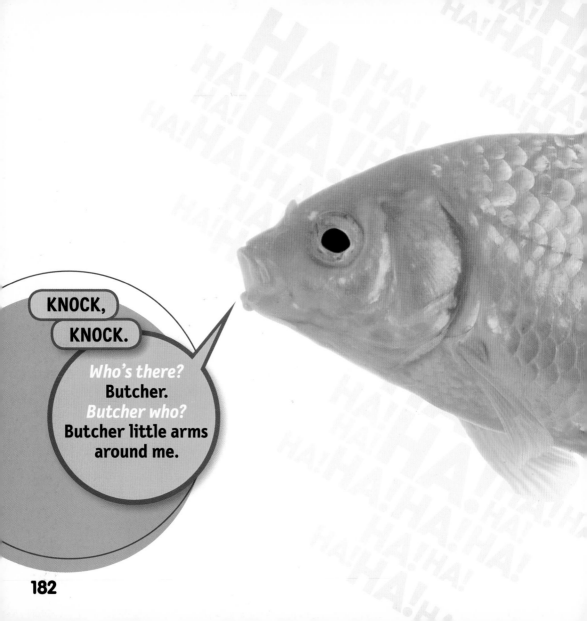

182

If a goldfish is left in the dark for a long time, it will turn almost white.

183

TONGUE TWISTER!

Say this fast three times:

Preshrunk silk shirts.

Q What gets **smaller** when you turn it **upside down?**

A The number 9.

Q What did the judge say when the skunk walked into the room?

A "Odor in the court."

Q What is the worst kind of driving school?

A The one that offers crash courses.

Q What gets **wetter** the more that it **dries?**

A A towel.

Q Why didn't the skeleton go to the dance?

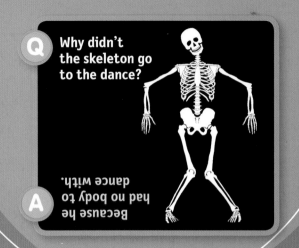

A Because he had no body to dance with.

Q Why did the turtle cross the road?

A To get to the Shell station.

Wolf guenon monkeys have cheek pouches to carry food as they travel.

187

This shop stocks

socks with spots.

KNOCK, KNOCK.

Who's there?
Vampire.
Vampire who?
Vampire State
Building.

The beluga whale is
one of the smallest
species of whale.

Q Why can't your nose be 12 inches long?

A Because then it would be a foot!

Q Why did the boy sprinkle sugar on his pillow?

A So he could have sweet dreams.

Q When does a **cart** come **before** a **horse?**

A In the dictionary!

Q How do you know that carrots are good for your eyesight?

A Have you ever seen a rabbit wearing glasses?

Q What is the **center** of gravity?

A The letter V.

Q Who are a hamburger's favorite people?

A Vegetarians.

Q What looks like half a tomato?

A The other half.

Q Why did the **belt** go to jail?

A Because it held up a pair of pants.

Double-crested cormorants are strong swimmers and divers.

KNOCK, KNOCK.

Who's there?
Beezer.
Beezer who?
Beezer black and yellow and make honey.

193

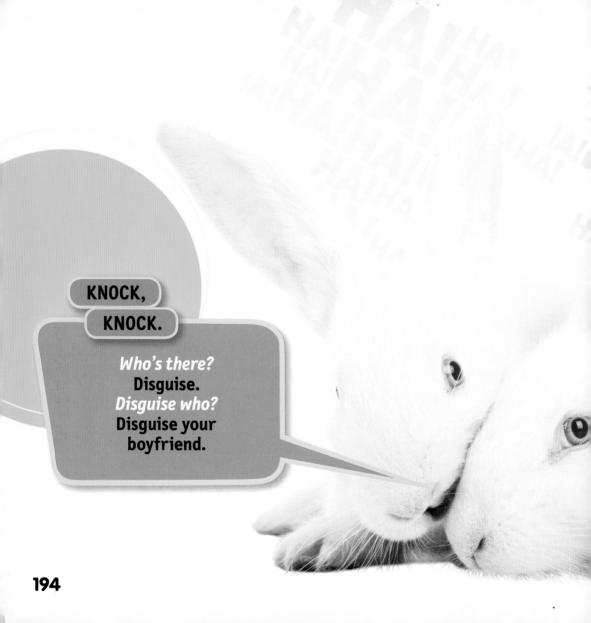

194

A rabbit's
teeth never
stop growing.

Mountain goats are not true goats; they are actually goat-antelopes.

KNOCK, KNOCK.

Who's there?
Truffle.
Truffle who?
Truffle with you is that you're too shy!

196

Say this fast three times:

Thieves seize skis.

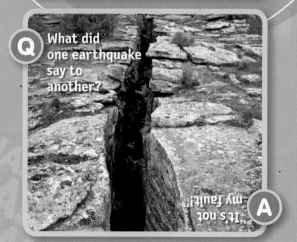

Q What did one earthquake say to another?

A "It's not my fault!"

197

Say this fast three times:

Sixish.

Q What do frogs drink?

A Croak-a-cola.

Q Why didn't the **hot dog** star in the **movies?**

A Because the rolls weren't good enough.

What did the **big** firecracker say to the little firecracker?

"My pop is bigger than yours."

Now **that** was funny!

JOKEFINDER

T

TONGUE TWISTERS

ILLUSTRATIONCREDITS

Cover: (chimpanzee), Richard Stacks/Index Stock Imagery/Getty Images; Back Cover: (rollercoaster) Carl R. Mukri; (cow) smereka/Shutterstock; (Just Joking cover) Winfried Wisniewski/zefa/Corbis; 4-5, Ron Kimball/KimballStock; 6, Mitsuaki Iwago/Minden Pictures; 7 (Top), Josh Randall/Dreamstime; 7 (Bottom), Mantonino/Dreamstime; 8 (Top, Left), Darlyne A. Murawski/National Geographic Image Collection; 8 (Top, Right), Carlos Caetano/Shutterstock; 8 (Bottom, Left), Sparkia/Dreamstime; 9, Alex Hyde/Minden Pictures; 10-11, Giancarlo Liguori/Shutterstock; 12 (Top), Koch Valerie/Dreamstime; 12 (Bottom), Denise Kappa/Dreamstime; 13, Jason Mintzer/Dreamstime; 14, Heather A. Craig/Shutterstock; 15 (Top, Left), Andrey Kiselev/Dreamstime; 15 (Top, Right), Olinchuk/Shutterstock; 15 (Bottom, Left), Bartosz Wardziak/Dreamstime; 16-17, Jezper/Shutterstock; 18, Gerard Lacz/Minden Pictures; 19, Alexei Novikov/Shutterstock; 20 (Top, Left), Outdoorsman/Dreamstime; 20 (Top, Right), ludovic rhodes; 20 (Bottom, Left), Vladimir Zheleznov/Dreamstime; 21, Kevin Schafer/Minden Pictures; 22-23, fivespots/Shutterstock; 24, Winfried Wisniewski/Minden Pictures; 25 (Top, Left), David Acosta Allely/Dreamstime; 25 (Bottom, Left), biburcha/Shutterstock; 25 (Bottom, Right), Catherine Ledner/Getty Images; 26 (Top, Left), Tetiana Novikova/Dreamstime; 26 (Bottom, Right), David Evison/Shutterstock; 27, Biosphoto/Cyril Ruoso; 28, Valentina_S/Shutterstock; 28 -29, Ambient Ideas/Shutterstock; 30, Musat Christian/Dreamstime; 31, Vladimir Melnik/Shutterstock; 32 (Top, Left), Guy J. Sagi/Shutterstock; 32 (Top, Right), smereka/Shutterstock; 32 (Bottom, Left), Audrey Snider-Bell/Shutterstock; 33, Michael Elliott/Dreamstime; 34-35, Johan Swanepoel/Shutterstock; 36, Tropper/Shutterstock; 37 (Top, Left), Ljupco Smokovski/Dreamstime; 37 (Bottom, Right), Kruchankova Maya/Shutterstock; 38 (Top), basel101658/Shutterstock; 39, Tom Soucek/Alaska Stock LLC; 40-41, JIANG HONGYAN/Shutterstock; 42, Eric Isselée/Shutterstock; 43 (Top, Left), Johan Swanepoel/Shutterstock; 43 (Bottom, Left), Matteo photos/Shutterstock; 43 (Bottom, Right), Sharon Dominick; 44, Theo Allofs/CORBIS; 45, Anastasija Popova/Shutterstock; 46-47, szefei/Shutterstock; 48 (Top, Left), MindStorm/Shutterstock; 48 (Top, Right), 2001 Twentieth Century Fox/ZUMA Press; 48 (Bottom, Right), szpeti/Shutterstock; 49, Don Hosek/Shutterstock; 50, Simon Litten/Minden Pictures; 51 (Top, Left), Jperagine/Dreamstime; 51 (Top, Right), Worachat Sodsri/Shutterstock; 51 (Bottom, Left), Shutter1970/Dreamstime; 52, Juliya_strekoza/Shutterstock; 54, Omar Ariff Kamarul Ariffin/Dreamstime; 55, Karamysh/Dreamstime; 56 (Top, Left), Glock33/Dreamstime; 56 (Bottom, Right), Stanislav Duben/Shutterstock; 57,

Gallo Images/SuperStock; 58-59, Vasyl Helevachuk/Shutterstock; 60, Steffen Schellhorn/FotoNatur; 61 (Top, Left), iconico/Shutterstock; 61 (Top, Right), Brandon Alms; 61 (Bottom, Right), DM7/Shutterstock; 61 (Background), Donnarae/Dreamstime; 62, Ron Chapple/Dreamstime; 63, Derrick Neill/Dreamstime; 64-65, Chuck Rausin/Shutterstock 64-65 (Background), hkeita/Shutterstock; 65, ethylalkohol/Shutterstock; 66, Karl Terblanche/ardea; 67 (Bottom), Eric Isselée/Shutterstock; 67 (Bottom, Right), Danny Smythe/Shutterstock; 68 (Top, Right), Orla/Shutterstock; 68 (Bottom, Left), Sadeugra; 68 (Bottom, Right), gualtiero boffi/Shutterstock; 68 (Background), Maitree Laipitaksin/Shutterstock; 69, Mark Thiessen/NGS Staff; 70-71, Kirsanov/Shutterstock; 72, Michio Hoshino/Minden Pictures; 73 (Left, Center), Olga Chernetskaya/Dreamstime; 73 (Bottom, Right), Moomsabuy/Dreamstime; 74 (Top, Left), Oliver Hoffmann/Shutterstock; 74 (Bottom, Right), Jodi Kelly/Dreamstime; 75, Tom Grill/Corbis; 76-77, Eduard Kyslynskyy/Shutterstock; 78, Suzi Eszterhas/Getty Images; 79 (Top), AJYI/Shutterstock; 79 (Bottom), Sabino Parente/Shutterstock; 80 (Top, Left), Jacek Chabraszewski/Dreamstime; 80 (Top, Right), Thyrymn/Dreamstime; 81, Isselee/Dreamstime; 82-83, Aurinko/Dreamstime; 84, Ocean/Corbis; 85 (Top, Right), sarah2/Shutterstock; 85 (Bottom, Left), Eric Isselée/Shutterstock; 86 (Top), Dmitrijs Dmitrijevs/Shutterstock; 86 (Bottom), Tropicdreams/Dreamstime; 87, Toby Sinclair/Nature Picture Library; 88-89, Hintau Aliaksei/Shutterstock; 90, Comstock/Getty Images; 91 (Top, Right), Guido Vrola/Dreamstime; 91 (Bottom, Left), Maisna/Shutterstock; 91 (Bottom, Right), Kathy Burns-Millyard/Shutterstock; 92 (Bottom, Left), Subbotina/Dreamstime; 92 (Bottom, Right), Kharidehal Abhirama Ashwin/Shutterstock; 92 (Background), Joan Kerrigan/Shutterstock; 93, Lisa F. Young/Dreamstime; 94-95, Rich Carey/Shutterstock; 96-97, Nagy-Bagoly Arpad/Shutterstock; 98, Michael Kern/Visuals Unlimited/Corbis; 99 (Top), Jiri Hera/Shutterstock; 100 (Top, Left), Robert Pernell/Shutterstock; 100 (Top, Right), think4photop/Shutterstock; 100 (Bottom, Left), Yury Shirokov/Dreamstime; 101, Sergemi/Dreamstime; 104, Gary Vestal/Getty Images; 105 (Top, Left), Jag_cz/Shutterstock; 105 (Bottom, Right), Ed Phillips/Shutterstock; 106 (Top, Left), Graham Stewart/Shutterstock; 106 (Bottom, Left), Kamenetskiy Konstantin/Shutterstock; 106 (Bottom, Right), Toy boat in waterpool/Shutterstock; 106 (Background), Elena Blokhina/Shutterstock; 107, Eleonora Kolomiyets/Shutterstock; 108, Jurgen & Christine Sohns/Minden Pictures; 109 (Top), zirconicusso/Shutterstock; 109 (Top), Susan Flashman/Shutterstock; 109 (Bottom), diez artwork/Shutterstock; 109 (Background), Anelina/

Shutterstock; 110-111, Hinrich Baesemann/dpa/Corbis; 112, ARZTSAMUI/Shutterstock; 113, Amanda Melones/Dreamstime; 114-115, Tish1/Shutterstock; 116, IMAGEMORE Co., Ltd./Alamy; 117 (Top), Melinda Fawver/Shutterstock; 117 (Bottom), Africa Studio/Shutterstock; 118 (Top, Right), Viorel Sima/Shutterstock; 118 (Bottom, Left), Ah Teng/Shutterstock; 118 (Bottom, Right), Ronen/Shutterstock; 119 (Left), vitor costa/Shutterstock; 119 (Right), Eric Isselée/Shutterstock; 120-121, Eric Isselée/Shutterstock; 122, Lynn M. Stone/Nature Picture Library; 123 (Top), Yusuf YILMAZ/Shutterstock; 123 (Bottom, Left), Sharon Dominick; 123 (Background), Iakov Kalinin/Shutterstock; 124 (Top, Left), Canoneer/Shutterstock; 124 (Top, Right), allegro/Shutterstock; 124 (Bottom, Left), ilFede/Shutterstock; 124 (Bottom, Right), Louella938/Shutterstock; 124 (Background), Iaroslav Neliubov/Shutterstock; 125, Mike Flippo/Shutterstock; 126, s_oleg/Shutterstock; 127, Eric Isselée/Shutterstock; 128, Tom & Pat Leeson/ardea; 129 (Top), viki2win/Shutterstock; 129 (Bottom), Carl R. Mukri; 130 (Top, Left), John Lund/Getty Images; 130 (Top, Right), zkruger/Shutterstock; 130 (Bottom, Right), TsuneoMP/Shutterstock; 131, James Phelps Jr/Dreamstime; 132 -133, VitCOM Photo/Shutterstock; 134, Teine/Dreamstime; 135 (Top, Left), Peter Blazek/Shutterstock; 135 (Top, Right), Booka/Shutterstock; 135 (Top, Right), Szasz-Fabian Ilka 135 (Bottom, Right), W. Scott/Shutterstock; 135 (Bottom, Right), ene/Shutterstock; 135 (Background), gibsons/Shutterstock; 136 (Top), Christopher Elwell/Shutterstock; 136 (Bottom), Nattika/Shutterstock; 137, Tonnyx/Dreamstime; 138-139, Marzanna Syncerz/Dreamstime; 140, Chris Lorenz/Dreamstime; 141 (Top, Left), Rosli Othman/Shutterstock; 141 (Top, Left), Heizel/Shutterstock; 141 (Top, Right), MANDY GODBEHEAR/Shutterstock; 141 (Bottom, Left), kedrov/Shutterstock; 141 (Background), Sergieiev/Shutterstock; 142 (Top, Left), Chris Harvey/Shutterstock; 142 (Top, Right), Ellen Morgan/Shutterstock; 142 (Bottom, Right), Richard Goldberg/Shutterstock; 143, Eric Isselée/Shutterstock; 143 (Bottom, Right), mexrix/Shutterstock; 144-145, pandapaw/Shutterstock; 146, RTimages/Shutterstock; 147 (Right), dcwcreations/Shutterstock; 148, National Geographic Image Collection/Alamy; 149 (Top), dragon_fang/Shutterstock; 149 (Bottom), Bine/Shutterstock; 150 (Top, Left), Teeratas/Shutterstock; 150 (Top, Left), Esterio/Dreamstime; 150 (Top, Left), Tomica Ristic/Shutterstock; 150 (Bottom, Right), Hannamariah/Shutterstock; 151, aleks.k/Shutterstock; 154, Ingo Arndt/Nature Picture Library; 155 (Top), Picsfive/Shutterstock; 155 (Bottom), Mike Flippo/Shutterstock; 156 (Top, Left), 3DDock/Shutterstock; 156 (Bottom, Right), Ragnarock/Shutterstock; 157, Regien Paassen/Dreamstime;

160 (left), Danny Smythe/Shutterstock; 160 (right), Mny-Jhee/Shutterstock; 161 (Top, Left), John Orsbun/Shutterstock; 161 (Top, Right), ra3rn/Shutterstock; 161 (Bottom, Left), Eric Isselée/Shutterstock; 162 (Top), Robert Adrian Hillman/Shutterstock; 162 (Bottom), Nordling/Shutterstock; 163, Roger De Montfort/Dreamstime; 165 (Front), Lightspring/Shutterstock; 165, design56/Shutterstock; 166, Hoberman Collection/SuperStock; 167 (Bottom), rangizzz/Shutterstock; 167 (Bottom, Right), ruigsantos/Shutterstock; 170 (Bottom, Left), Pichugin Dmitry/Shutterstock; 170 (Top, Right), tunart; 170 (Top, Right), Kuttly/Shutterstock; 170 (Bottom, Right), Sharon Dominick; 171 (Left), Suzanne Tucker/Shutterstock; 171 (Right), Steve Cukrov/Shutterstock; 172, Graeme Pitman; 173 (Top, Left), Christophe Testi/Shutterstock; 173 (Top, Right), ajt/Shutterstock; 173 (Bottom, Left), saiva_l/Shutterstock; 174 (Top, Left), Kelly Cline; 174 (Bottom, Right), Marina Jay/Shutterstock; 175, Eric Isselee/Shutterstock; 178, Cathy Keifer/Dreamstime; 179 (Top), Ugorenkov Aleksandr/Shutterstock; 179 (Top), Maridav/Shutterstock; 179 (Bottom), Vlue/Shutterstock; 180 (Top, Right), StudioSmart/Shutterstock; 180 (Bottom, Left), Piotr Pawinski/Dreamstime; 181, DavidYoung/Shutterstock; 184, 101imges/Shutterstock; 185 (Top, Right), Eric Isselée/Shutterstock; 185 (Bottom, Left), Nikiandr/Shutterstock; 186 (Top), vadimmmus/Shutterstock; 186 (Bottom), objectsforall/Shutterstock; 187, Hotshotsworldwide/Dreamstime; 190, Petar Zigich/Dreamstime; 191 (Top, Left), Adrian Assalve; 191 (Top, Right), Jakub Krechowicz/Shutterstock; 191 (Top, Right), Oleg Sytin; 191 (Bottom, Right), Maks Narodenko/Shutterstock; 192 (Top, Right), Sukharevskyy Dmytro (nevodka)/Shutterstock; 192 (Bottom, Left), Pixel Embargo/Shutterstock; 193, Steve Byland/Dreamstime; 196, Dejan Smaic/Rex/Rex USA; 197, Lee Prince/Shutterstock; 198 (Top, Right), Molnár Ákos/Shutterstock; 198 (Bottom, Left), marco mayer/Shutterstock; 198 (Bottom, Right), Cherkas/Shutterstock; 199 (Left), digitalconsumator/Shutterstock; 199 (Bottom, Right), Jaap2; 202, Richard Stacks/Index Stock Imagery/Getty Images; 152- 153, Dmitriy Karelin/Shutterstock; 158-159, Christian Musat/Shutterstock; 164-165, jocic/Shutterstock; 164-165 (Bottom), jocic/Shutterstock; 168-169, Alex White; 176-177, Andrea Danti/Shutterstock; 176-177 (Background), Triff/Shutterstock; 182-183, v.s.anandhakrishna/Shutterstock; 188 -189, Cole Vineyard; 194-195, Viorel Sima/Shutterstock; 200-201, Suzi Eszterhas/Minden Pictures

National Geographic Kids would like to thank the following people for their invaluable expertise:

Robert Pascocello, *Scientific Assistant, Department of Herpetology, Division of Vertebrate Zoology, American Museum of Natural History*
Erin Stahler, *Biological Science Technician, Yellowstone Wolf Project*
Travis W. Taggart, *Director, Center for North American Herpetology*
Gaylene Thomas, *Animal Care Supervisor, San Diego Zoo*

Published by the National Geographic Society
John M. Fahey, Jr., *Chairman of the Board and Chief Executive Officer*
Timothy T. Kelly, *President*
Declan Moore, *Executive Vice President; President, Publishing and Digital Media*
Melina Gerosa Bellows, *Executive Vice President; Chief Creative Officer, Books, Kids, and Family*

Prepared by the Book Division
Hector Sierra, *Senior Vice President and General Manager*
Nancy Laties Feresten, *Senior Vice President, Kids Publishing and Media*
Jonathan Halling, *Design Director, Books and Children's Publishing*
Jay Sumner, *Director of Photography, Children's Publishing*
Jennifer Emmett, *Editorial Director, Children's Books*
Carl Mehler, *Director of Maps*
R. Gary Colbert, *Production Director*
Jennifer A. Thornton, *Director of Managing Editorial*

Based on the "Just Joking" department in
***National Geographic Kids* magazine**
Kelley Miller, *Senior Photo Editor*
Julide Dengel, *Designer*

Staff for This Book
Robin Terry, *Project Editor*
Eva Absher-Schantz, *Managing Art Director*
Lisa Jewell, *Photo Editor*
David M. Seager, *Art Director/Designer/Editor*
Grace Hill, *Associate Managing Editor*
Joan Gossett, *Production Editor*
Lewis R. Bassford, *Production Manager*
Susan Borke, *Legal and Business Affairs*
Kate Olesin, *Associate Editor*
Kathryn Robbins, *Design Production Assistant*
Hillary Moloney, *Illustrations Assistant*
Michaela Berkon, Molly Gasparre, Carly W. Larkin, *Editorial Interns*

Manufacturing and Quality Management
Phillip L. Schlosser, *Senior Vice President*
Chris Brown, *Vice President, Book Manufacturing*
George Bounelis, *Vice President, Book Production*
Nicole Elliott, *Manager*
Rachel Faulise, *Manager*
Robert L. Barr, *Manager*

The National Geographic Society is one of the world's largest non-profit scientific and educational organizations. Founded in 1888 to "increase and diffuse geographic knowledge," the Society works to inspire people to care about the planet. National Geographic reflects the world through its magazines, television programs, films, music and radio, books, DVDs, maps, exhibitions, live events, school publishing programs, interactive media and merchandise. *National Geographic* magazine, the Society's official journal, published in English and 33 local-language editions, is read by more than 38 million people each month. The National Geographic Channel reaches 320 million households in 34 languages in 166 countries. National Geographic Digital Media receives more than 15 million visitors a month. National Geographic has funded more than 9,400 scientific research, conservation and exploration projects and supports an education program promoting geography literacy. For more information, visit nationalgeographic.com.

For more information, please call 1-800-NGS LINE (647-5463) or write to the following address:

National Geographic Society
1145 17th Street N.W.
Washington, D.C. 20036-4688 U.S.A.

Visit us online at nationalgeographic.com/books

For librarians and teachers: ngchildrensbooks.org

More for kids from National Geographic: kids.nationalgeographic.com

For information about special discounts for bulk purchases, please contact National Geographic Books Special Sales: ngspecsales@ngs.org

For rights or permissions inquiries, please contact National Geographic Books Subsidiary Rights: ngbookrights@ngs.org

Paperback ISBN: 978-1-4263-1016-4

Library ISBN: 978-1-4263-1017-1

Printed in China
12/TS/1